Journey with
Joseph
Through Advent

Samuel G. Schaefer
illustrated by Kyla Wiebe

Siretona
CREATIVE

Journey with Joseph through Advent © 2022 Samuel G. Schaefer

www.schaeferbooks.com/

Published by Siretona Creative • www.siretona.com

Schaefer, Samuel G., author.
  Journey with Joseph through Advent / written by Samuel G. Schaefer; illustrated by Kyla Wiebe

English version
  978-1-988983-55-4 (Softcover / Paperback)
  978-1-988983-66-0 (Hardcover)
  978-1-988983-56-1 (eBook)

German translation by Johanna Wiebe
  978-1-988983-57-8 (Softcover / Paperback)
  978-1-988983-67-7 (Hardcover)
  978-1-988983-59-2 (eBook)

Ukranian translation by Inna Dmytriieva
  978-1-988983-58-5 (Softcover / Paperback)
  978-1-988983-69-1 (Hardcover)
  978-1-988983-60-8 (eBook)

Russian translation by Inna Dmytriieva
  978-1-988983-61-5 (Softcover / Paperback)
  978-1-988983-68-4 (Hardcover)
  978-1-988983-62-2 (eBook)

Interior design and layout by Julie Karen • www.juliekaren.com
Cover design by Kyla Wiebe and Colleen McCubbin

Distributed to the trade by The Ingram Book Company

Contents

A Note to Parents

As a father of two sons, I wrote this book to tell my children the story of the Savior entering the world.

I chose to tell the story from the view of Joseph and put some of my own reactions to situations into the story.

I also wanted to create a way to tell my sons about their family and what their parents have experienced in their life. To help with this, I've included questions after every day to engage the children in talking about their lives and their parents lives.

May this book help you to pour love into your own children or other people in your life.

Samuel Schaefer

A Note to Children

Each December many people celebrate—children, parents, good and not-so-good friends. They celebrate something special that happened over 2000 years ago. Not everyone knows how that celebration started, nor fully knows what it means. Some people only celebrate because everyone else does.

So I want to tell you the story of how it all started and, more importantly, what it means.

Thankfully, when it happened there were people who kept a record and wrote down the details. Because they did all that work, we can read about it over and over again. That way we won't forget its life-changing and life-giving meaning and we can help each other remember. We need to remember, especially this story and many others in those texts, which we call the Scriptures, because they are telling us something we all should know and never forget.

Every day, from now until Christmas, we will have a little part of that wonderful story for you, with something extra for you to talk about.

TALK ABOUT IT

For example, ask the person who reads to you if there is something
that happened in their life that they do not want to forget.
Ask them to tell you that story and then listen well.
Maybe someone can even write down that story,
so you can read it and never forget.

Joseph

Hi there, I am Joseph. I am from a group of people called the tribe of Judah in the land of Israel. Some of my forefathers have been great kings who ruled this country. Lots of people still talk about those kings and how good those days were. I am not a king like my forefathers. The time when one of my people was a king has long been gone.

The Romans have come into our country! They are very strong and powerful people. We must obey and listen to them. The Romans are telling my people how we must live.

I am a builder now. I build houses and can help people if they break something. I always have work. Sometimes I like to think about how it would be if I were a king and did not have to build houses. But those thoughts are dangerous now. It is better not to tell anyone about them. We must accept the Romans as our kings. I don't really like it, but it could be worse.

Guess what? I found someone special. She is such a great person and I want to marry her. Her name is Mary and thinking of her makes everything look better.

TALK ABOUT IT

Did you ever have to live through a hard time?
How did you get through it? Maybe the person reading
to you can share about a time like that in their life.

Mary

Did I tell you about Mary yet? She is a treasure. She comes from the same people as I do, the people of Judah.

Coming from the same people means that at one point we had the same father, and guess who that was? He was the great King David, who was an outstanding fighter. Because he trusted God, he fought against the giant, Goliath. At that time, David was a little guy and was not yet the king. But King David lived a long time ago and so Mary and I aren't that closely related anymore.

In my culture, it really helps if you want to get married to someone from the same people, because the parents arrange the marriage and this makes for a faster agreement. I had to ask my parents to talk to Mary's parents. Sometimes marriages are arranged before the couple even knows each other. So it is very important to have the blessing of the parents, otherwise it disturbs not just the families but also the whole community you are living in.

Mary cares about people and what happens to them. She is very good at understanding how people think and what they need and she can make tasty soup! I am so glad we are officially engaged and we can get ready to get married.

TALK ABOUT IT

What do you know about the kind of family your parents are from? Maybe the one reading to you can help you retell it.

DAY
3

Elizabeth

Mary just left to see some people from her family. She went to go and see Elizabeth.

Mary said Elizabeth is having a baby and she needed to go and help her.

Elizabeth is married to a priest named Zechariah who was chosen to do a very special work for God. He was allowed to go into the temple and be in the presence of God. I am having goosebumps just thinking about it. People have died in the presence of God. When he came back out of the temple after being in the presence of God, he could not say a word.

Well, now Mary is with Elizabeth, helping her with the baby. I'm not sure how long she will stay there. All I know is that Elizabeth is not young anymore and having a baby at her age can be dangerous and take a lot of strength. It makes sense that Mary wanted to be there to help. I think it is a good thing. Mary will learn so much about babies and can hear from Elizabeth herself. This will be a good experience for her because we want to have children, too! Sadly, our children won't be allowed to work in the temple as they will belong to the people of Judah. But it looks like it can be dangerous to work in the temple, so maybe that is a good thing.

TALK ABOUT IT
Ask the one reading to you to tell you about some of the special work that has been done in your family.

Mary Coming Back

Mary is back. I was surprised to see her. Suddenly there she was! But something had changed.

As I greeted her, Mary told me about a miracle that happened. After Elizabeth had the baby and everyone came over to hear the name of their new son, Elizabeth's husband started to talk again. What a surprise! Zechariah hadn't spoken a word since he came out of the presence of God and now he spoke again. Apparently, God closed Zechariah's mouth because he didn't believe what an angel told him while he was in the temple. The angel said that Elizabeth would be having a baby and they should call him John. But Elizabeth's husband didn't believe it, so God prevented him from speaking.

It isn't the first time a man couldn't believe that his wife would have a child. A very long time ago, our forefather Abraham was promised by God that he would have his very own son and that through him there will be even more children than the stars in the sky. It was a journey for Abraham to believe that it would be his own son. At the end, Abraham believed God so much that he was willing to give his son back to God. He knew God could bring his son back from the dead to keep his promise.

TALK ABOUT IT
How easy is it for you to believe?
Maybe the one reading to you can tell you of a time
when they chose to believe in God's promises.

DAY
4

DAY 5

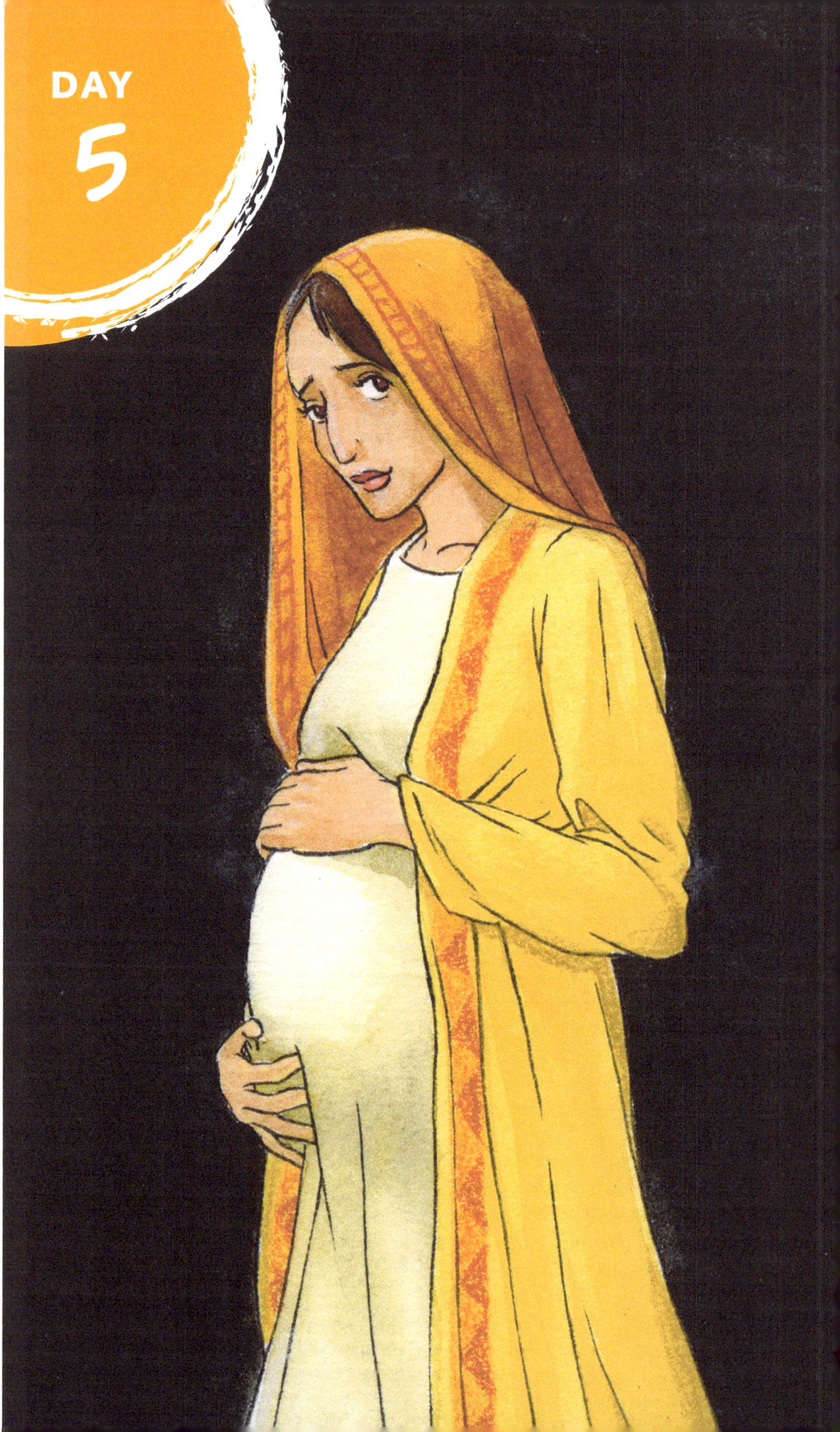

Mary is having a Baby

This is some bad news. Soon everyone in town will know.

Mary just told me that she is having a baby. I can't believe it. How can she have a baby with someone else? Even so, I believe we are meant to be together. Everything is planned for us to get married, but now she is expecting a baby. I don't know what I should be doing now. I could talk to her parents about this and maybe we can find a way out of this situation. Everyone will talk about how we couldn't wait until we were husband and wife. But it isn't even my baby. Why should I still get married to her?

I can't tell the leaders of our town, because they will punish her for not keeping the agreement not to have a baby with someone else. They might even kill her. I have heard about others that this happened to. I don't want this to happen to Mary, but why did she decide to have a baby without me?

This is a disaster. Maybe I could just disappear and leave Mary with her parents. Then she can explain the situation she brought upon us. Maybe that is what I should be doing. That way no one will be punished.

TALK ABOUT IT
Do you think it is easy to speak the truth?
Is it better to leave a problem and hope it will get better?
Maybe the person reading to you can share
about such a dilemma in their own life.

Mary's Side of the Story

Did I tell you Mary's explanation about how she is having a baby?

Mary said that before she left for Elizabeth's place to help with Elizabeth's baby, an angel came and visited her. She said that this angel told her she would have a baby boy. He said she should call him Jesus and he would be called the Son of the Most High and he would be a king from the throne of David—the king where both my family and Mary's family connect again. But the angel also told her that this baby will be such a great king that he will be king forever.

Right then I wasn't so sure anymore if I could believe Mary, the one person I wanted to have a family with. But the craziest thing is that Mary said she asked the angel how this could all be possible because we weren't married yet. And the angel told Mary that the Holy Spirit would make sure that there will be a baby growing inside of her. I couldn't believe it.

Mary asked me what she should have done. She said she could only say to the angel that she was God's servant and it shall happen as he told her. I don't think I said anything. What could I say?

TALK ABOUT IT

Have you ever had a dream about God or angels
when you were sleeping?
Maybe the one reading to you can tell
of a story how God led them.

Joseph Obeys

Angels are real! Last night I went to bed after packing and getting ready to disappear. While I was sleeping, an angel talked to me and said that I, a son of David, should not be afraid to stay with Mary and that I should go ahead and become her husband. The baby she has is from the Holy Spirit and I should give the baby boy the name Jesus, because he will save his people from their sin.

That was very scary. I don't want to be like Elizabeth's husband, not believing, and then perhaps lose my voice or something.

The crazy part is what the angel said at the end. He said the baby's name should be Jesus because he will save his people from their sin. This could only mean that this baby will be the promised Savior, the one who will be like Moses, saving his people out of the country where they have been slaves and leading them into the promised land. In the same way, this baby Jesus will lead us out of our sins!

If those words are true then Mary's baby will be the prophet and Savior we all have been waiting for from the beginning of this world, already promised by God in the garden of Eden!

TALK ABOUT IT
Do you know what sin means?
Why it is important to have someone save you from it?
Maybe the one reading to you can help you understand.

Listening and Obeying

I did it. I spoke with Mary. I told her about the angel I saw and what he told me and that I believe her now.

Mary was very happy to hear that I believe her and that we can get married. This will be a very special time for us. We will celebrate for a whole week, which is how our people celebrate a wedding. And then Mary and I will be officially husband and wife. That way our baby has a father and Mary has a husband and the people cannot talk badly about Mary anymore.

People will still talk, but for now, let's get ready for our wedding. There is so much to do. We need the food to eat and the wine to drink, enough for all those days. We need musicians to play so we can dance. And I need to get my place ready so Mary can come and live with me.

This will be the start of our family. Like I told you, I need to obey the angel. I don't want to lose my voice like Elizabeth's husband did. I'd better believe and obey and do exactly as the angel has told me.

TALK ABOUT IT

Do you like to obey and do as you are told, even though it might not look like a good thing for you right now? Maybe the person reading to you can share about a time they chose to obey even though it was difficult.

News from Rome

We are married! But something is going on. Soldiers from Rome have come into town. They brought news from Caesar Augustus, their leader. He is the one that sent all the soldiers to make us listen.

I went to the center of the town to hear more news. Usually, there isn't any good news coming from Rome. They almost always want more money or more of the food that we have planted. Well, this time they were talking about this new idea Caesar Augustus had. Everyone has to go to the town where their family is from so that Rome can count how many people are living in their kingdom.

This is crazy! That kind of action can lead to trouble. One time, King David wanted to know how many men were living in his kingdom. After he counted the men, God brought a punishment on the people and many died. God would provide victory over his enemies no matter how strong they were. Therefore, the king was never to count how many fighting men there were in his kingdom, but always trust in God's strength.

The orders from Caesar Augustus are a problem. Our forefather, King David, is not from here. We are from Bethlehem, so now we have to make it all the way to Bethlehem before Mary has the baby.

TALK ABOUT IT

Do you know where your family came from
and why your family lives were they live now?
Maybe the person reading to you can help you
answer that question.

Walking to Bethlehem

I have talked to Mary and, as I thought, she had a hard time accepting that we have to walk all the way to Bethlehem. I did not need to tell her why. She knew we had to go, because if we didn't the soldiers would make us. And she also knew that there wasn't much time left to get to Bethlehem, because the baby could be born on the road if we waited too long.

I can understand why Mary was upset with all this. I don't like it either, having to walk all the way to Bethlehem just because Caesar Augustus wants to know how many people live in our land that he claims to be his.

What helped Mary is that I said I would do everything I could to make this work. I told her I would organize this journey, even get a donkey. Not sure if I will find someone who would give us one for this journey. Donkeys are really important and it is hard to buy one and even harder to find someone who will lend you one.

It will work out because this baby is from God, so God will give us what we need to get to Bethlehem. Guess what? Those thoughts came from Mary, not from me. I admire her for her faith.

TALK ABOUT IT

Maybe the person reading to you can tell you
about a time in their life when they had to go
and do something that seemed impossible.

DAY
10

Looking for a Place

We made it! This was a different journey. We don't even know how long we should be staying here, but probably we will stay for some time. Back home they are talking not so nice about us, because Mary had a baby in her tummy before we were married. But here no one knows, and no one needs to know. We are married and we have family here in Bethlehem.

We had almost no problems on the road. We knew we needed more time walking to Bethlehem, but there were lots of people on the roads because of this new law that everyone had to go to the place where their family was from. Some people walked with us for a while and some people helped us carry things for a few miles. The best thing was that for every night we had a place to stay. I knew it would be challenging to walk with Mary all this way because of the baby, but we made it. We just had to take it slower than we were both used to.

The biggest surprise came when we arrived in Bethlehem. There are lots of people here. I told you, my family is large, but people are used to having family stay over and making space for more.

TALK ABOUT IT

Do you know of anyone who was looking for a place to live and how they found a place to stay? Maybe the person reading to you can tell their story about someone who helped them.

The Birth Place

We found a place to stay in Bethlehem! I am thankful, being with family. But I realize now that the baby is wanting to come out, and we can't have it with all the people staying in the same room.

In our culture, it makes everyone unclean being with someone who has given birth to a baby. Becoming unclean means you are not able to take part in any celebrations or going to meetings. So I am going to ask the shepherds outside of Bethlehem if we can have the baby in a room in the tower of the flock. It's a room on the ground floor of a tower that overlooks the area where all the sheep are eating.

In this room the shepherds bring all the sheep that are about to have lambs. When the sheep give birth to their lambs, the shepherds catch the lambs before they hit the ground. They wrap them in cloths and put them in the manger, so they won't be able to hurt themselves. They need to make sure that it doesn't get any scratches and stays perfect. Then the priests from the temple come to choose the perfect lamb for a sacrifice. That is why the room is always kept very clean.

TALK ABOUT IT

So many things have meaning. Are there some things you do because they have a meaning, like praying before you go to bed or to school? Maybe the person reading to you can explain you some of those meaningful rituals.

DAY
12

DAY
13

The Birth of Jesus

The shepherds agreed to our plan! They had no problem and understood our situation.

Mary and I are now in a room in one of those towers. It is very clean! The shepherds have a whole system for how to keep it warm in here. I have been prepping this place for a couple of days and now I brought Mary out here as well, as she started to feel the baby wanting to come out. But I forgot to bring anything to wrap the baby in. I hope Mary brought the cloths that she prepared for the baby to be wrapped in. There are many clean cloths that we can use over here if she forgot them. I feel so bad. I should have thought of them. She worked so hard on those cloths, to decorate them with the symbols from our tribe of Judah. They are really beautiful.

Oh wait, it's happening! Mary is calling! The baby is coming out!

Wow! What a small little baby! I forgot how small a baby can be. This is unbelievable! I wrapped him in the cloths and he fell asleep right after he ate. I laid him in the manger now, where he is safe and protected.

TALK ABOUT IT

Did anyone tell you how it was when you came into this world?
And maybe even what time it was?
Maybe the person reading to you can tell you those details.

The Shepherds Find Jesus

I had a very difficult time sleeping last night. First, I was really excited that our son is now here, and second, Mary needed rest and I tried to give her space as much as possible.

Something unbelievable happened! I thought we would be fine sleeping through the night and just feeding our son every now and then. But in the middle of the night, after I put our baby boy back into the manger, I heard many voices coming towards us. I went outside to check and suddenly I was surrounded by all the shepherds.

I didn't know how they knew about our baby being born, but here they were, running like it was their baby. They said they came to see Christ the Lord their Savior, and insisted on seeing the baby and worshipping him. So I let them come in and put a light over our son's head.

And then, the shepherds started to pray and say that it was true what the angels had said. I am not sure what they were talking about, so I let them talk. They were thankful that their Savior finally arrived and they were allowed to be the first to see him.

Oh, I have to go! Our son is crying. I will tell you about the angels tomorrow.

TALK ABOUT IT

Wow, the shepherds found Jesus! How happy are you
when you finally find something you have been looking for?
Maybe the person reading to you can tell how
they found Jesus or how you can.

DAY
15

The Shepherds and the Angels

Unbelievable! The shepherds told me about angels coming to them in the middle of the night. Shepherds tend to tell stories to pass their time. But not all shepherds are like that. A long time ago, my forefather King David was a shepherd here. David loved to sing while watching the sheep.

They said the reason they came to see Jesus is that while they were watching the sheep, out of nowhere an angel appeared. They were afraid seeing an angel like that, right in front of them.

Then the angel said to them that they didn't need to be afraid. The angel was bringing good news of great joy for all the people: the Savior had been born for them in the town of Bethlehem—the Messiah, the Lord. And the angel gave them a sign to know which baby it was: he would be wrapped in cloths and lying in a manger.

That is what the angel said and that is why the shepherds were so sure it was our son, because we wrapped him in cloths and laid him in a manger. Then the shepherds said that all of a sudden there were many more angels who started to sing.

They sang, "Glory, glory in the highest place and on earth be peace to the people that his favor rests on."

TALK ABOUT IT

That message to the shepherds was a big announcement! Maybe the person reading to you can tell you how they received an important message and how that made them feel.

The Shepherds and the Passover Lamb

The angel also told the shepherds, "The Savior has been born to you in the town of Bethlehem. He is the Messiah, the Lord." They slowly realized this meant a great deal.

Because the angel mentioned that the Savior would be wrapped in cloths and lying in a manger, the shepherds thought of their own lambs, which would be born right here in this room, and how every year the High Priest from the temple comes to pick out the perfect lamb to be the Passover Lamb.

At the Passover feast, we remember the last night our people spent in Egypt where they had been slaves. On that night, everyone was asked to take a perfect lamb, kill it, put the blood on the doorposts, prepare the lamb, and eat it. An angel was coming to everyone who didn't put the blood over the door, and the angel brought death to the firstborn son of the house. That is also why our forefathers could leave Egypt, because even the son of the king of Egypt died.

It's a horrible story. But we are still remembering it every year, because God saved my people. The blood of the lambs had saved the oldest sons of our people in Egypt, and now there is another Savior wrapped in cloths but this time it's not a lamb but a little human.

TALK ABOUT IT

Do you wonder why you are doing certain things,
like lighting the candles during Christmastime?
Maybe the one reading to you has some examples as well.

DAY

17

The Shepherds Follow the Call

The shepherds showed up in the middle of the night at our place and wanted to see Jesus. They saw Jesus in the manger wrapped in cloths, in the same way their lambs would usually lay there. And then they fell on their knees and thanked God for sending our son, their Savior.

After the shepherds left, they talked to everyone they saw about finding the Savior. They are still talking to everyone about the angels who came and the message they received. They tell everyone about the Passover Lamb and how it relates to our baby.

The shepherds also started to talk about the Scriptures we all know, like the one where it says that the prophet we are all waiting for will do more miracles than Moses did. Then they started to talk about a song King David wrote, where he sings about the Savior being like a tree planted by streams of water, which yields its fruit in season and whose leaf does not wither. That whatever he does prospers, and he will be strong and courageous, and he will build a new kingdom.

All of the Scriptures talk about a Savior coming. What will happen if those shepherds do not stop talking? Maybe everyone will just think they are crazy and not even listen to them any longer.

TALK ABOUT IT

Have you ever heard such wonderful news that you couldn't stop talking about it and thanking God for it? Maybe the one reading to you can share of such an occasion.

The Mark

Our son is now seven days old and we are preparing for this special day tomorrow. We will circumcise our baby on the day he is eight days old. I know that circumcise is a strange word. It means that our son will have a mark that will show him that he belongs to our people, the people God has chosen. We will have to cut a little bit of skin off. That way our son will always remember.

Not that he will remember this exact day, but he will know when he sees the skin missing that he belongs to our people. This is the sign God wanted the father of our people, Abraham, to have, and all his children, so we would know we belong to God. Only the boys will have this sign.

We also give the baby boys their name at this time. The angel told us that we are to give him the name of Jesus because he will save his people from their sins. Looks like Jesus will make a big difference in people—not through cutting off some skin, but by changing their heart when he saves them from their sin. And at that time it will not just be for the boys but for everyone!

TALK ABOUT IT

Do you have any special celebrations when a baby receives its name or around the time a baby is being born? Maybe the person reading to you can share of how your name was chosen.

DAY
19

Presenting Jesus at the Temple

We went to the temple in Jerusalem to give an offering so Mary could be considered clean again. We offered a pair of doves as we didn't have a lamb to offer. Also we paid five shekels of silver because Jesus is our first son.

There is lots of meaning attached to a firstborn son. He belongs to God, and we must give something for him in the temple. We are also to remember the time all those firstborn sons died in Egypt before our fathers left. The Egyptians didn't obey God when he asked them to put the blood of the lamb on the doorposts.

When we were at the temple, there was this old man and this old woman who talked to us. God had promised the old man, Simeon, that he would see the Savior before he died. Simeon said something that made Mary and I wonder. He said God would now allow him to die, because he finally have seen the salvation from sin that God has prepared for all people—for both the people of Israel and for all the other nations.

Now that Mary is considered clean, we can move back into Bethlehem. I am really wondering what else will happen and who else we will meet!

TALK ABOUT IT

Do you know that there is a purpose for everyone living on this earth like Simeon described the purpose of Jesus? Maybe the person reading to you can help you find that purpose.

The Wise Men Come

Jesus is about to start walking now and just the other day a large crowd came to Bethlehem. They told me they came from far away in the East to worship the king, and they knew about the king being here because of the star leading them to my house.

When I heard that, I thought about those shepherds that came when Jesus was born. I wonder who will be next to come and worship Jesus!

All the visitors came into the house because they really wanted to see Jesus, and you know what? They started to worship Jesus like the shepherds did!

Maybe we needed to be reminded who our son Jesus really is. Those men are actually very important. They are wise men who help their king make good decisions. That is why they came with soldiers and so many other people helping them.

A trip like this doesn't just happen. These men came because their king allowed it and saw it as something important. And all this because of a star that they had never seen before. This star was so important that they had to search for its meaning. And that is why they are here.

TALK ABOUT IT
It is something to celebrate every time a child is born.
Maybe the person reading to you can tell you who
came to see you when you were born.

DAY
20

DAY

21

The Star

I asked those wise men about that star, because I know the star story from our father Abraham. God told our father Abraham that his children will one day be as many as the stars in the sky. And now one of those stars is so special to those wise men!

The wise men saw this special star in the sky and it wasn't like any other star. It was a very special star they had never seen before. So they started to read all kinds of writings to know if the appearance of a star like this was mentioned.

One day they came across the writings of our people and there they found this text: "A star shall come out of Jacob, and a scepter shall rise out of Israel." That is why they started to think about Israel. Then they read that Judah will be the tribe of Israel that will hold the scepter, which means being a king. Right after they understood all of that, they prepared to travel to Jerusalem because that city is the capital of Judah.

When the wise men left Jerusalem, they told me they saw the star again, the same star they had seen in their country. The star was leading them directly here. They came to our place because of the star.

TALK ABOUT IT

Isn't it interesting what can lead you to someone special like Jesus? Maybe the one reading to you can tell you their story of finding someone or something special.

The Gifts

The wise men told me that nothing like this star has ever been reported and to see such a star is like seeing a miracle. For them, it made sense that this star was announcing a king—or even more than a king.

That is also why they brought us three special gifts. The first gift was gold, which is for a king. The second was frankincense, which the priests use in the temple for a food offering, which gives the offering a pleasing aroma to God. Third, they brought myrrh. I am not sure why they brought him that gift. It is usually used to put on people when they are dead and going to be put into a grave.

They came from far away and it took them many days to get here. Preparing for the journey and having enough soldiers for protection and helpers for the men is not a small thing for the king to allow. But the wise men only had to tell their king about that miraculous star. They came and gave Jesus these special gifts, hinting towards what the future would bring for Jesus' life.

TALK ABOUT IT

Did you know that it's probably because of the wise men
that we give gifts to each other at Christmastime?
Those gifts had a lot of meaning.
Do your gifts have meaning too?
Maybe the one reading to you can help you
bring meaning to the gifts you give.

DAY

22

Herod

The wise men didn't come right to Bethlehem. I guess they stopped in Jerusalem first, because that is where all our kings have lived through time.

They told me they went right to Herod, the king of this area, and asked him about the baby that had been born. There is no one Herod would allow to be king besides himself and then those important men came all the way suggesting there was another king.

So, Herod the king was angry and called some of the teachers who teach the Scriptures to us, and he asked if there is anything written that talks about where the Christ would be born. And our teachers told him that it is written that Bethlehem in the land of Judah is an important town because out of it will come a king who will be the shepherd of God's people. That was written by a man called Micah seven hundred years before Jesus was born.

Herod talked to the wise men privately and asked them when the star appeared the first time. He asked them to come back after they found Jesus, so he could go and bring him gifts as well. Is Herod really going to come to see Jesus, too?

TALK ABOUT IT

How easy is it to believe in writings like the one from Micah? Micah's words were written seven hundred years earlier. Maybe the one reading to you can share with you about promises that are written in Scripture, too.

Dreams

The wise men are packing up and leaving right away. They just told me they had a dream. They saw it as a warning not to go back to Herod and tell him about where he could find Jesus.

Herod made it very clear to them that he wanted to know where the royal baby was born, and sent the wise men on a mission to give him all the information about the baby they would find.

I had a dream too. An angel spoke to me and said: "You need to escape. Get up and take Jesus and Mary to Egypt. Stay there until I tell you to come back, because Herod is going to search for Jesus to kill him."

Mary, Jesus, and I are going to Egypt right away. We are not telling anyone. We must run away fast. I am glad the wise men gave us all those gifts. Those gifts will help us while we are trying to hide in Egypt. This is almost like Abraham or Jacob and his family, who went to Egypt to survive.

Maybe we must go to Egypt because of those Scriptures, like the one where it says that God will call his son out of Egypt. Those words are from the prophet Hosea, also written about seven hundred years ago before Jesus was born.

Hopefully no one knows that we are going to Egypt.

TALK ABOUT IT

Running away isn't fun. Did you ever run away from someone? Maybe the person reading to you can share of a situation like that.

DAY

24

DAY
25

Back in Town

We stayed in Egypt a long time, but we are back in Israel now.

You might be surprised to hear that we are in Nazareth and not in Bethlehem. Well, Bethlehem went through a difficult time because of Herod after we ran away, and we didn't really want to be a reminder of that time. Also, where we are now is not in the same area that King Herod's son rules over. He became king over the same area after his father died. Most importantly, it is because of a warning from an angel that we settled here and not in Bethlehem.

While we were still in Egypt an angel told us to go back home. He said to me, "Get up, take the child and his mother, and go back to Israel." We didn't know that Herod had died, but we had to do what the angel told us. When I arrived close to Bethlehem, I learned that Herod's son was now king and I got really scared. Then an angel warned us again and so we came back here to Nazareth.

What a journey, starting in Nazareth with an angel speaking to Mary and now coming back to Nazareth because an angel told us to. I think there is a reason for this, maybe another writing about Jesus the Savior. It is unbelievable how many writings there are that talk about the Savior coming. I think one teacher told me there are between 350 and 500 writings. We will see if they all come true. No wonder God has to send angels to make sure it all happens exactly as it is written. That is also why we can trust those things written in the Scriptures!

TALK ABOUT IT

Believing that Jesus is the Savior, promised a long time ago, was not easy at that time and is not easy today. Do you want to get to know Jesus? Maybe the person reading to you can help you. If no one can tell you, just ask God to help you get to know his son Jesus. He will send you someone who will help you.

Conclusion

Jesus came back to Israel from Egypt. When he was about thirty years of age, he started a ministry proclaiming that the Kingdom of God had come. He walked and preached and did many miracles so the people started to believe that he was the promised prophet, the prophet that was like Moses.

Jesus taught twelve men very closely about the texts of the Jews and everything that needed to happen. He explained to them that everything that was written in the Scriptures must happen. It is written that the Savior will suffer and rise from the dead on the third day and preach in his name to all nations, starting with Jerusalem.

Another author named Paul wrote to a young man named Timothy that the Scriptures, which he knew from childhood, helped him see how he could be saved through faith in Christ Jesus.

Jesus came so we all could be saved, understand God's great plan, and believe in Jesus, his son. We are to ask God the Father to help us understand, through the texts of the Scriptures, why Jesus had to come and why he is our salvation. Jesus is the son of God and he said that he is the only way to God, his Father, and whoever believes in him will have eternal life.

Thank you for reading. May God the Father draw you to Jesus so that you may believe, receive the Holy Spirit, and have eternal life with the Father in heaven. See you there!

Notes

DAY 1 Joseph
+ **Matthew 1:1–17** shows the promised line through Joseph.
+ **1 Kings 10:23–29** is a little description of King Solomon's riches and power.

DAY 2 Mary
+ **Luke 3:23–38** is believed to be the genealogy through the bloodline of Mary.

DAY 3 Elizabeth
+ **Luke 1:1–23** is the account of the angel speaking to Zechariah in the temple.
+ **Luke 1:36–40** tells how Mary went to see Elizabeth, her cousin.

DAY 4 Mary Coming Back
+ **Luke 1:57–66** talks about the account of Zechariah talking again.
+ **Genesis 16:1–2** Abram listened to his wife and did not believe the promise of God as before.

DAY 5 Mary is having a Baby
+ **Matthew 1:18–19** shows that Joseph wanted to divorce Mary quietly.

DAY 6 Mary's Side of the Story
+ **Luke 1:26–39** lets us see the angel's visit to Mary.

DAY 7 Joseph Obeys
+ **Matthew 1:20–23** is the account of the angel visiting Joseph.
+ **Deuteronomy 34:10–12, Acts 3:22, Acts 7:37** are about waiting for a prophet greater than Moses.

- **Exodus 3:6–10, Exodus 12:50–51, Exodus 14:28–31**, **Deuteronomy 34:1–4** are accounts of Moses being used by God to save his people from Egypt and leading them into the Promised Land.

DAY 8   Listening and Obeying

- **Matthew 1:24–25** shows that Joseph did exactly as the angel of the Lord commanded him.
- **John 8:31–42** The Pharisees argue with Jesus about who is his father and theirs.

DAY 9   News from Rome

- **Luke 2:1–3** tells about Caesar's decree that everyone needed to be registered.
- **2 Samuel 24:10–17** tells the account about David counting his fighting men against God's wishes and then a plague kills 70,000 men of the population.
- **1 Samuel 16:4–13** David was a son of Jesse who lived in Bethlehem.

DAY 10   Walking to Bethlehem

- **Leviticus 12:6–8** People could offer two turtledoves if they could not afford a lamb.
- **Luke 2:24** Joseph and Mary offered two turtledoves, which means they where probably poor and couldn't afford a donkey to ride on.

DAY 11   Looking for a Place

- **Luke 2:6–7** The word "inn" can also be translated as "guestroom." It makes sense that if there is family around, you would always stay with family or friends of the family, but there was no separate place for Joseph and Mary to go through childbirth and keep everyone else "clean."

DAY 12   The Tower of the Flock

- **Micah 4:8** mentions the tower of the flock and that kingship for Jerusalem should come to it.

DAY 13   The Birth of Jesus

+ **Luke 2:7** mentions the birth of Jesus and that they wrapped him in swaddling clothes and laid him in a manger.

DAY 14   The Shepherds Find Jesus

+ **Luke 2:15–17** shows the shepherds going to see Jesus laying in the manger.

DAY 15   The Shepherds and the Angels

+ **Luke 2:8–14** is the account of the angels appearing to the shepherds.

DAY 16   The Shepherds and the Passover Lamb

+ **Exodus 12:21–32** tells the story about the first Passover in Egypt.

DAY 17   The Shepherds Followed the Call

+ **Luke 2:17–20** we can see how everyone wondered about what the shepherds told them and that Mary treasured up all these things in her heart.
+ **Deuteronomy 34:10–12** talks about waiting for a prophet greater than Moses.
+ **Psalm 1** lets us see the perfect person who walks according to the Scriptures.

DAY 18   The Mark

+ **Luke 2:21** is about Jesus' circumcision and name-giving.
+ **Genesis 17:9–14** is the command from God to Abraham to circumcise all his offspring as a sign of the covenant between God and Abraham.

DAY 19   Presenting Jesus at the Temple

+ **Luke 2:22–38** tells of the visit to the temple for purification and presenting the firstborn.
+ **Leviticus 12:1–8** is an account of the purification process after childbirth for a woman to be considered clean again.

+ **Exodus 13:11–16, Numbers 3:11–13** and **Numbers 18:15–16** tells us how the firstborn would belong to God and they would need to be redeemed for a price.

DAY 20   The Wise Men Come
+ **Matthew 2:1–2** and **2:9–11a** show us how the wise men came to worship the king.

DAY 21   The Star
+ **Matthew 2:2** and **Matthew 2: 9–10** tell the account of how the star appeared.
+ **Genesis 15:5–6** is the account of God promising Abraham offspring like the stars in the sky.
+ **Numbers 24:17** talks about a star coming out of Jacob and being a scepter out of Israel.
+ **Genesis 49:10** is the first promise that points to Jesus coming out of the tribe of Judah.

DAY 22   The Gifts
+ **Matthew 2:11** describes the gifts the wise men brought to Jesus.

DAY 23   Herod
+ **Matthew 2:1–8** tells the account between the wise men and King Herod in Jerusalem.
+ **Micah 5:2** is the reference that Matthew quotes in the account of Herod and the wise men talking about where the Messiah will be born.

DAY 24   Dreams
+ **Matthew 2:12–15** shows us that Joseph and Mary went with Jesus to Egypt.
+ **Hosea 11:1** is the reference that Matthew uses about God calling his son out of Egypt.

DAY 25 Back in Town

+ **Matthew 2:16–23** tells us about Herod killing babies in Bethlehem, and about Joseph, Mary, and Jesus returning to Nazareth.

CONCLUSION

+ **Matthew, Mark, Luke,** and **John** all share about the ministry of Jesus.
+ **Luke 24:44** is Jesus teaching that everything in the Scriptures must be fulfilled.
+ **2 Timothy 3:15** talks about the Scriptures which make people wise for salvation (help them see how they could be saved through faith in Christ Jesus).
+ **John 3:16** Jesus himself declares that whoever believes in him shall have eternal life.
+ **Acts 10:43** explains how all the prophets witness that whoever believes in Jesus will have forgiveness of sins through him.

Learn more

To learn about our translations, order more books, donate copies for refugees, and more, visit our website:

www.schaeferbooks.com

Thank you

To my wife Bonita who planted the seed.

To my nieces who inspired this book.

To Colleen McCubbin and everyone at Siretona Creative who helped me make this book into what it is now.

To Kyla Wiebe for her art and patience with my ideas.

To my two sons who listened to me reading them this book throughout the years.

To friends and family who have been an encouragement thoughout this process.

To all the translators and editors who have helped me so far and will help me publish this book in other languages.

www.ingramcontent.com/pod-product-compliance
Lightning Source LLC
Chambersburg PA
CBHW040905120626
46551CB00006B/646